A Good Life

A Good Life

Frederica Steinberg

DAMIANOS PUBLISHING · 2023

© 2023 Frederica Steinberg. All rights reserved.
No part of this book may be used or reproduced by any means, graphic, electronic or mechanical, including photocopying, recording or taping, or by any information storage retrieval systems without the express written permission of the publisher, author and/or illustrator.

Cover and many interior photos by the author — others by family and friends, included with thanks. An earlier version of this book was printed privately in 2023, in a small edition for distribution to family members and friends.

Library of Congress Control Number: 2023923032
ISBN 978-1-94157-356-3 (hardcover)
ISBN 978-1-94157-357-0 (paperback)

Published by Damianos Publishing
2 Central Street, Studio #152
Framingham, MA 01701 USA
DamianosPublishing.com

Produced through Silver Street Media by
Bridgeport National Bindery,
Agawam, MA USA
First printed 2023

This book was printed on paper from sources committed to rigorous forest management standards, developing, and promoting sources of renewable energy, using recycled fiber and materials, and promoting forest certification in the U.S. and around the world. SFI (Sustainable Forestry Initiative), and FSC (Forest Stewardship Council).

(FSC Certification ensures that products come from responsibly managed forests that provide environmental, social and economic benefits to those forestry areas. The FSC Recycled label indicates that the product was made from 100% recycled materials.)

For Daniel and Alex

Contents

A Good Life	3
The Experts	4
Bookmarks	4
The Bernadini Tomb	5
1962	7
Love	7
The Piano	8
Driving	9
The Puddle	11
Our Japanese Garden	12
Midnight	13
Hunkering Down	15
The Rainbow	16
Dinner	18
The No-Longer-Do List	19
I Liked It	21
Breakfast	22
Words	23
Wind	23
Smiling Motorcycles	24
Obits	26
The Manuals	29
Arthur	30
Learning	31
Will You Forgive Me?	32
The Brain	33
Tai Chi	33

In the Woods	34
The Trash Cans	36
The Acorn	37
So Long	38
The Wedding Veil	39
The Period	40
Lionel Messi	42
Opapa	42
I See You	43
What More Can I Ask?	44
A Broken Lamp	45
Often Almost	45
Blankets	46
Knickers	47
Philosophy 101	49
Schindler's List	50
I Miss You	51
Two Burly Kind Men	52
Tears	54
Will It Hurt?	57
Oak Leaf, February 2023	58
Pile of Ashes	59
Wedding Ring	60
Three Plastic Containers	62
April 3, 2023	65
Guilt and Relief	66
Not Yet	67
Peace	68

A Good Life

A Good Life

In our little apartment on
the second floor with a balcony
overlooking the Janiculum Hill.

Gamboni, our landlord,
a nice enough guy,
sometimes gruff.
He smoked a cigar.

Living room with rattan furniture,
one bedroom, one bathroom,
a tiny kitchen with table and
two blue wooden chairs.

I learned how to cook
pasta carbonara
and *fegato alla Veneziana*
in that kitchen.

I remember the cool tile floors,
the leaky bathroom faucet,
the French doors that
opened onto our balcony.

We drank Chianti
on that balcony watching the
Italian sun disappear.

We had a good life.

The Experts

"Dementia," I ask the doctors.
"Can you treat it? Can you slow it down?"

Probably not, say the learned doctors
white coats with pens in their pockets
stethoscopes draped around their necks.

And who are we to question the experts?
Dementia 101.

Bookmarks

He sat, knees crossed,
reading Max Weber
or *Cycle World*.

Sometimes Ann Sexton,
Kafka, Ezra Pound
and Henry James.

On this couch, he plowed
through *Moby Dick*
and smiled through histories
of Titian and Venice.

That was then.
Now the bookmarks
no longer move.

The Bernadini Tomb

Our romance flourished
in the Bernadini Tomb
outside Rome in Palestrina.

The chill of the hard stone.
The cold sarcophagus.
But warmed by the blood
that coursed through our veins.

"Do you remember this?"

You tilted your head and
squeezed out that naughty
smile of yours.

1962

"Sixty years of marriage is a long time."
He sits on the couch smiling at me
wondering what I'm talking about.

He shakes his head, bewildered.

"Honey," I say, "we married
in 1962. Do you remember?"

His smile widens.

Love

Love caresses the ring
on my finger
and says "thank you" for
your delicious bowl of risotto.

The Piano

Your deft fingers rolled across
the piano keys
never missing a note.

Beethoven, Bach,
Chopin and Liszt.
Or four hands with Henry
Ehrenreich.

Now Middle C
is a mystery.

Driving

We talked to the doctors
who cautiously led us down
the driving road.

Maybe Arthur should not
drive anymore.

The dents in the car
speak volumes.

The Puddle

The rain comes down
   and makes a puddle
      that quietly waits for me

to look down at your face, not mine,
   and see the familiar gap
      between your teeth.

My fingers
   stroke your wet cheek.
      Thank you, puddle, for this Gift.

Our Japanese Garden

I hope you don't mind.

I cut down the three
remaining crab apple trees
that surrounded the Japanese Garden
you and I built twelve years ago.

They were sick with fungus,
wilted and blackened leaves
and trunk cankers.

Like you, their time had come.

Midnight

"I'm going shopping in the Upper Valley,"
he tells me.

He sits in the car with the engine going.
"It's midnight. Everything is closed," I say.

He frowns and knits his brow.
"Yes, it's midnight," I repeat.

"Oh," he says. "Midnight?"
"Yes," I say again.

He turns off the car, and I open his door.
"Let's return to the house," I suggest.

We slowly walk across the lawn,
holding hands.

Hunkering Down

It used to be this way.

We began to hunker down
when the leaves turned copper
and fell to the ground
chattering among themselves.

Your warm hand
circled mine as we
walked from outbuilding
to outbuilding
closing doors
and returning shovels to
their rightful places
in the tool shed.

And piled the porch furniture
in the pick-up
complaining all the time
because that damn wooden table
was so heavy.

Now I hunker down,
but I hunker down alone.

The Rainbow

"Arthur, can you see the rainbow
draped over the mountain?"
Here for only a few fleeting moments.

Like you.

Dinner

We sit in silence
listening to our forks
and knives
scrape against the plates.

I watch him push
his food onto his fork
with his fingers.

The peas fall off.
He carefully picks each up
and replaces it.

He saws his chicken thigh
back and forth
with his knife.

I look out the glass slider
at the darkening sky.
It's mid-October around 6:30.

And things will get darker,
I know.

The No-Longer-Do List

"Don't get lost," I remind you
as you start up the hill.
"Just follow the red tape."

But you didn't follow the red tape
and you did get lost.

I guess we'll have to add
one more thing to the
No-Longer-Do List.

I Liked It

I liked it when you put on your galoshes
    and shoveled the front deck and filled
        the canvas log carrier with wood for our stove
            and returned with snow stuck to your beard.

I liked it when you sat by the maple tree watching me
    mow the lawn with a huge smile on your face
        and a twinkle in your eyes
            and that soft way about you.

I liked it when you were alive.

Breakfast

"Are you dressed?" It's 11:00 A.M.
No response.
Still sitting in the chair at the foot of the bed
staring out the window
where I'd left him an hour ago.

"Arthur, can I help?"
He nods and looks at me.
I pull the stocking up
and help him with the other one.
I lift one foot and slip it into his shoe,
then the other and tie the laces.
It's now noon.

I leave the room for the kitchen
and make his breakfast.
Orange juice, toast, two fried eggs.
"Arthur! Breakfast is ready!"
No response.
It's now 12:30.

I return to the bedroom.
He hasn't budged.
"Arthur, breakfast is on the table."
He looks at me and asks,
"Breakfast?"

Words

I search for words
that reveal
this place where
I've never been.

But am now.

Wind

The wind blows across my bow
     switching its course
          from time to time
              and shifting its strength.
       I feel its sting and shout —
   it softens just a bit to let me
catch my breath.

Smiling Motorcycles

You no longer spend hours in
the motorcycle barn
the way you used to
sitting on the red milk carton
covered with oil and grease
tinkering with the bikes,
your sons surrounding you
learning and laughing and
gathering tools and following
your instructions.

The motorcycles no longer smile
because they know
you've forgotten what to do.

Obits

Your absence is more present
these days.

You sit on the couch,
your Bic pen in your
plaid shirt pocket,
reading the *Valley News*.

You flip to the Obits,
like you always do – first.

You read yours, smile, and turn to the
sports section.

The Manuals

Alex made sure the Gold Star
had been restored in time
to be on display for your memorial service
on June 18, 2022.

Photographs hung on the walls
of the horse barn.
A few forged hooks, some pocket watches,
a wrench and a hammer sat on the workbench.

Your brocade vest, made by me,
and one of your flamboyant neckties
were draped on a wire hanger
along with a red t-shirt and worn baseball hat.

One shelf held some of your
hundreds of books about metallurgy,
Chinese history, American crafts, Venetian
painting, ancient Greece, John Harrison, and travel.

Whoops! We forgot the manuals,
a favorite of yours.
Will you forgive us?

Arthur

Arthur was your name.
ARTHUR.
Two syllables.
Two vowels.
Four consonants.

Is that all that's left?

Learning

I didn't know it
when you sold our tractor
and the brush hog
and eight motorcycles
and some books
and a few other
odds and ends.

The check had already been made out
before I caught on.
The new owner beamed.
It wasn't his fault.
It was mine
for not keeping an eye
on things.

But I did catch on
and made sure you kept
that helmet with the dents
and our sons' old motorcycle boots,
bent and worn and brittle,
and the sit-down mower.

I was new at this dementia business.

Will You Forgive Me?

Do I expect too much?

I ask you again to wipe the dishes
and you just
sit there and stare
at Mt. Ascutney
and the tall maple that
hovers outside
the window.

Am I too mean?

I ask you ten times to
carry out the trash
and it's still sitting there
full of empty milk cartons
and soiled paper napkins
and rotten chicken bones.

Do I expect too much?
Maybe.

Will you forgive me?

The Brain

Some or many of the ninety billion
neurons rebelled
and dementia
snuck in unannounced
tightening its sneaky grip
like the dreaded Python.

Not a happy poem.
But it's not a happy life
right now.

Tai Chi

What happened?
Why are you dressed?
Five days a week for twenty-five years
you practiced Tai Chi every
morning at 7:00.

You took weekends off
but today is Thursday.
What happened?

"I don't know," you say.
And that was that.

In the Woods

I open the front door and yell.
No answer. Where is he?
Maybe I need to check the cellar —
once more.

No luck.

I quickly walk to the horse barn,
now filled with old furniture and tools.
"Arthur!" Silence.
I check each stall, now empty, and the
tack room, where the croquet
and badminton sets now live.

No luck.

The motorcycle barn? No.
The forge? No.
The pool house? No.

Arthur! Arthur! Silence.

"Hmmm," I say out loud.
"Should I panic? Not yet."
He's not in the house,
he's not in the outbuildings.
Where else could he be?

My eyes suddenly fall on the Kubota.
Maybe I'll find him in the hay field?
The Kubota and I head down the hill,
searching left and right.
No Arthur.
No body.
Nothing.

I notice a hawk soaring above the house.
Was this a sign?

Dementia hit Arthur hard.
Old habits disappeared,
bookmarks stopped moving.

Maybe I'll find him in the woods.

The Trash Cans

Arthur returned with four
huge trash cans teetering in
the bed of the red pick-up.

I only needed one small one.

"Did you read the list?"
I asked.
"List? What list?"

The Acorn

The beautiful smooth brown acorn
keeps me company
when I think of you.
I found it in your blue jeans pocket,
the blue jeans with the frayed cuffs
and the red suspenders
that held them up
because your thin body had
lost its shape.

So Long

Darling, is it time for me to say goodbye?
I've been avoiding this
for seven months
but eight months seems right.

I'm walking in the wind
tucking my unruly hair
behind my ears
something you always did

with your right hand,
fingers arranging
the hair neatly
where it belonged.

Goodbye is as untidy a word as my hair.
So maybe it's not goodbye, but so long…

The Wedding Veil

Pausing is a good thing to do
from time to time
to gather my straying thoughts.

I wonder where you are.
Are you somewhere?
Or nowhere?

Maybe you're in my wedding veil.

The Period

We lived with no punctuation
for years
the days and nights
leapt forward
bringing joy and laughter

then slowly the commas arrived,
and we lingered
from time to time
to figure things out.

Soon came the semicolons;
we paused
longer and longer
and then the dreaded period
hit us.

A full stop.

Lionel Messi

You sat in your recliner
watching soccer
in your waning years
eyes glued to
Messi, Salah, Ronaldo,
and Neymar,
Liverpool, Chelsea,
Manchester City
and Barcelona.

"Oh shit!" You cried from your recliner.
Had Messi missed a goal?

Opapa

He was your father
that guy who waved his baton
at orchestras all over the world.
You didn't like him
you said.
He wasn't a good father to you
you said.
Now you listen to his tapes,
especially Bruckner's Eighth Symphony.
"Maybe he was a better
father than you remember —
or just a good musician?"

You say nothing.

I See You

I see you standing near the wall
that divides the two fields,
gazing at Mount Ascutney.

Or sitting on the deck
staring at noisy crows
flying overhead.

And swimming in the pool
wearing your rubber bathing
cap and black goggles.

Sometimes lingering in the stall
where Kaya stood quietly
while you tightened her girth.

Or in the kitchen when
you made oatmeal
with raisins and nuts.

Often on the couch
reading the *New York Times*,
Goethe or *Classic Bikes*.

And in our bed, your pillow
propped up while you read
Pablo Neruda.

What More Can I Ask?

You sit on the wooden bench
   under the fading maple tree
      and watch the black crow
         fly overhead and perch on
            the tippy top branch of
         our only oak tree.

And it's enough
   to put a twinkle back
      in your eyes.
         What more can I ask?

Nothing.

A Broken Lamp

I found him on the floor – again.
This time no cuts and stitches
just a bruised face
and a broken lamp.

Often Almost

Often is a loaded word,
as is almost.
But that's the way we live right now.
Often you fall.
Or you almost fall.
Or you often almost fall.

Blankets

Why do you sleep that way?
Your lower half off the bed,
legs dangling over the side.
I gently push your legs back
under the white sheet and blue blanket.

I never liked that blue blanket,
but you were partial to it.
I preferred the yellow one
that we could tuck in
at the end of the bed.
Ample, I'd say.

Sometimes I needed
to back off because
what's so important
about blankets
when so much more was at stake?

Knickers

Darling, I ask,
do you want to wear
your Levi's?

He stares at me.
Darling, I ask,
do you prefer your knickers?

Philosophy 101

You rode your Norton all over
Harvard Square and worked in
Tommy Jackson's
motorcycle shop instead of
attending Philosophy 101.

Learning about cylinder heads,
pistons, crankshafts,
camshafts, intake manifolds,
torque wrenches, flywheel pullers,
ball peen hammers and screwdrivers.

Finding the oil leak,
tightening the chains,
tuning a carburetor,
checking for sparks,
adjusting the points.

What's more philosophical than that?
Robert Pirsig would agree.

Schindler's List

Remember when . . .
outside in the cold
you wept after watching
Schindler's List?
I hugged you through your faded
navy L.L. Bean jacket.

You escaped Nazi Germany
but one uncle did not.
Were your tears for him?
Or for others?
Or maybe yourself?

Puzzled, you
furrow your brow.

I Miss You

I miss you lately
    not sure why
        it's been almost ten months
            since you died in that nursing home
            bedridden and vacant.

Your fingers lay flat against the sheet
    not moving when I gently placed my hand
        on top of yours
            squeezing hoping for some response
            but none came.

Two Burly Kind Men

I slowly opened the bathroom door.
And I was right to be frightened.

Arthur, naked and shaking,
sat on the closed toilet seat.
The heat was unbearable.
Why had he turned on the heat?

"Arthur, what are you doing?"
No eye contact, just mumbling.

What to do? Why hadn't he toppled over?
Had he completely lost his mind?
Should I call 911?

And I did.

The ambulance came one half hour later
and two burly, kind men gently
lifted Arthur off the toilet seat
onto a gurney.

It was cold outside;
only a thin blanket covered his body.
I added another to keep him warm
as the two burly, kind men lifted
the gurney and slid it into the
ambulance.

"May I come?"
"No," they said. "Come later,
after a doctor sees your husband."

Down the drive went the
ambulance with Arthur.

I walked back into the house
and made some coffee
and toasted a piece of 5-grain
bread. With jam.

It was 4:30 A.M.
on November 18, 2021.

I opened the curtains
waiting for the day to begin.
And it would begin
like every other day.

Tears

Tears are flowing today
because it's September 6, 2022,
our 60th wedding anniversary.

But you didn't make it.

I am wearing your old, creased Barbour jacket
with the grocery list
still in the pocket:
"bread, tomato, cuke, lime-lemon."
A short list.
"Olive oil" was crossed out.

Our hands touched in that wrinkled pocket.
Your wedding ring bumped up against
my finger.

Enough said.

Will It Hurt?

No, Honey, I will make sure
you won't have any pain.
He blinks into my face.

The nursing home provides
a bed and a few kind nurses,
boiled peas and fried fish.
Sometimes chocolate pudding.

No, Honey, I repeat;
dying won't hurt.
I kiss his forehead
and read him *Beowulf*.

Oak Leaf, February 2023

Today in Rock Meadow
I asked an oak tree for one of its
remaining thin delicate
curled brown leaves.

Yes, it said, so I gently snapped one from
its limb and cupped it in my hand
to protect it from the
blustery cold February wind.

The fierce wind also came
on Sunday, April 3, 2022
when I no longer could
hear your beating heart.

Pile of Ashes

You breathed one last breath on April 3, 2022.
The phone rang at 10:30 p.m.
"Is this Frederica Steinberg?"
"Yes," and I knew.

At midnight, the crematorium called.
"Is this Frederica Steinberg?"
"Yes," I said.
"Are we to pick up Arthur Steinberg?"
"Yes."

I walked around the apartment wondering
if Arthur would mind the terrible heat and fire
that would ravage his worn thin bony body.

A body that had climbed mountains
and apple trees
and barn roofs.

And his mind? Would that mind of his
melt in the furnace? Would its intellect escape?

And so it was that on April 4, 2022,
my husband of sixty years became
a pile of ashes.

Wedding Ring

When Alex picked you up
at the crematorium
he was given your gold
wedding ring
in a plastic Ziploc sandwich
bag.

End of story.

Three Plastic Containers

You sit on the mantel
in three plastic containers.
One is half full because
some traveled to Greece
in the pocket of Daniel's trousers
to rest on the ground
in front of the Parthenon
where you and I spent our first
honeymoon night
in a tent.

Do you remember that?
In a tent!
What were we thinking?

I'll join you when the time comes,
but not in a tent.

April 3, 2023

You died one year ago —
on April 3, 2022,
in the early evening.

I squeezed your hand and
kissed your cheek.
and said goodbye.

Your beard was rough,
and your hand quiet and still.
These things I remember.

And I recall your face,
Worn and thin and ready.
Enough, it said, enough.

We miss you, but you know that.
We loved you, but you know that, too.
And that's probably enough.

Guilt and Relief

Should I feel guilty because I'm relieved
that I'm free at last?
Free from being on call twenty-four hours a day?
Free from worry and stress?
Free from sleepless nights?
Free from driving you to appointments?
Free from picking you up off the floor
and worrying that I'll break a hip
because I've been diagnosed
with osteoporosis?

Friends wiser than I
say this is natural.
Say that guilt and relief
can live side by side —
comfortably.
Are you listening?
What do you think?

Because, after all,
you're free, as well.

Not Yet

April 3, 2023, was the anniversary
   of your death.

Your ashes wait patiently
   on the mantel in Vermont.

One day they'll lead
   me to your resting places.

But not yet.

Peace

Arthur, I need to let

you rest in peace . . .

release your hands,

both of them,

so you can settle in the wind,

the rain, the snow, the earth,

and . . . in our hay field.

A Good Life was composed in Bembo Book,
a modern interpretation of the types used by the
great Venetian printer Aldo Manuzio (c. 1450–1515).
Editorial counsel from Sally Brady. Design by
Bruce Kennett and Frederica Steinberg.